# ROME TRAVEL GUIDE

Essential Tips for First-Timers in Rome

by Francesco Umbria

© **Copyright 2021 - All rights reserved.**

The content contained within this book may not be reproduced, duplicated or transmitted without direct written permission from the author or the publisher.

Under no circumstances will any blame or legal responsibility be held against the publisher, or author, for any damages, reparation, or monetary loss due to the information contained within this book. Either directly or indirectly.

**Legal Notice:**

This book is copyright protected. This book is only for personal use. You cannot amend, distribute, sell, use, quote or paraphrase any part, or the content within this book, without the consent of the author or publisher.

**Disclaimer Notice:**

Please note the information contained within this document is for educational and entertainment purposes only. All effort has been executed to present accurate, up to date, and reliable, complete information. No warranties of any kind are declared or implied. Readers acknowledge that the author is not engaging in the rendering of legal, financial, medical or professional advice. The content within this book has been derived from various sources. Please consult a licensed professional before attempting any techniques outlined in this book.

By reading this document, the reader agrees that under no circumstances is the author responsible for any losses, direct or indirect, which are incurred as a result of the use of information contained within this document, including, but not limited to, — errors, omissions, or inaccuracies.

# Table of Contents

*Introduction* _____ *8*

*Chapter 1: Reasons to Love Rome* _____ *17*

    1) Rome Has Some of the World's Most Famous Historical Landmarks _____ 17

    2) You Can Experience an Exciting Part of World History While Touring Rome _____ 18

    3) You Will Get to Experience Some Fantastic Food While You Are in Rome _____ 18

    4) You Will Have the Opportunity to See Some Rare and Exotic Animals While Touring Rome _____ 19

    5) You Will Have the Chance to Explore Beautiful Ruins _____ 19

    6) There Are Some Wild, Exciting, and Amazing Things to See While You Are Here _____ 19

    7) You Will Have the Chance to Meet Some of the World's Greatest Artists While in Rome _____ 20

    8) You Will Have a Great Sense of History and Tradition While Touring This City _____ 20

    9) There Are So Many Different Ways that You Can Travel While in Rome _____ 20

    10) Going to Rome Will Provide You with an Unforgettable Experience _____ 21

*Chapter 2: Best Time to Visit* _____ *23*

    Spring _____ 25

    Summer _____ 26

    Autumn _____ 26

    Winter _____ 26

    Tips When Visiting Rome _____ 26

## Chapter 3: Rome's Must-See Attractions ... 33

   1. Colosseum ... 34

   2. Forum Romanum ... 35

   3. St. Peter's Basilica ... 35

   4. Piazza Navona and Campo de' Fiori ... 36

   5. Piazza del Popolo ... 36

   6. Pantheon ... 36

   7. Trevi Fountain ... 37

   8. Piazza del Popolo ... 38

   9. Palazzo della Civiltà Italiana ... 39

   10. Roman Forum ... 39

   11. Piazza Navona ... 40

   12. Campo de' Fiori ... 40

   13. Galleria Borghese ... 41

   14. Piazza di Spagna ... 41

   15. Piazza del Popolo ... 42

## Chapter 4: Beyond the Center: Unusual Things to Do in Rome ... 43

   Clothing Optional Beaches ... 43

   Michelangelo's House and a Tour of All His Works in the City ... 44

   Quirky Museum Openings ... 44

   Theatre Festivals ... 45

   Nocturnal Flights in a Hot Air Balloon ... 45

   Hidden Beer Garden at the German Embassy ... 45

   Drinking at a Fountain ... 46

   Pizza from a Hotplate ... 46

   Gelato in a Bath ... 46

   Food on Film at Rome's Open Air Cinema Festival ... 47

Theatre with a View _____ 47

Love on the Bridge at Villa Sciarra _____ 47

Epicurean Roof-Top Feast at the Hotel D'Italia _____ 47

Romantic Package with Aperitivo _____ 48

The Fountain of the Four Rivers _____ 48

The Portico d'Ottavia at Largo di Torre Argentina_____ 48

The Fountain of Apollodorus _____ 48

The Garden of Villa Medici _____ 49

Piazza del Popolo _____ 49

The Spanish Steps _____ 49

Castel Sant'Angelo _____ 49

Palazzo Laterano _____ 49

Piazza Venezia _____ 50

Sant'Ignazio Church_____ 50

San Lorenzo Maggiore_____ 50

Piazza Navona _____ 51

The Colonne di San Pietro_____ 51

Trajan's Markets _____ 51

The Riverbank _____ 51

Trajan's Forum _____ 52

The Cappella Arcivescovile _____ 52

The Pantheon _____ 52

Palatine Hill _____ 53

Colosseum _____ 53

St Peter's Basilica _____ 53

Santa Maria in Trastevere_____ 53

Piazza della Repubblica_____ 54

*Chapter 5: Eating in Rome* _____ 55

| | |
|---|---|
| Breakfast | 56 |
| Lunch/Dinner | 56 |
| Pizza & Pasta | 57 |
| Bars & Cafés | 58 |
| Snacks & Desserts | 59 |
| Dessert & Treats | 61 |

## Chapter 6: Rome After Dark — 63

| | |
|---|---|
| The Roman Pub | 64 |
| Night Clubs | 65 |
| The Theater | 66 |
| The Dance Hall/Live Music Club/Underground Club/Trance/House/Techno Club | 66 |

## Chapter 7: Drinking and Nightlife — 69

## Chapter 8: Shopping in Rome — 74

| | |
|---|---|
| Piazza di Spagna | 75 |
| Via Cola di Rienzo | 75 |
| Via Del Corso | 76 |
| Markets | 77 |
| What to Buy | 77 |
|     Clothes | 78 |
|     Leather Goods | 78 |
|     Jewelry | 78 |
|     Glass | 79 |
|     Food | 79 |

## Chapter 9: Rome with Kids — 80

| | |
|---|---|
| Best Museums & Sites for Kids | 80 |
| Top Tips | 81 |

## Chapter 10: Travel Tips — 83

| | |
|---|---|
| Arriving in Rome | 83 |
|     Leonardo da Vinci – Fiumicino Airport | 83 |

| | |
|---|---|
| Civitavecchia | 84 |
| Ciampino Airport | 84 |

## Getting Around — 84
Metro — 85
Tram & Buses — 85
Taxis — 88
Walking — 89
Bike Share — 89

## Shopping and Sights. 7 days — 90

## Book Your Stay — 92

## *Conclusion* — *93*

# Introduction

In a city founded on the banks of the river Tiber in 753 BC, many centuries have come and gone.

Throughout Roman history, many events have shaped the course of this prosperous metropolis: from its violent founding to destruction by war; from wars that were fought on her soil to those won overseas; from colonial expansion to eventual decline.

In more recent times, Rome has asserted itself as one of Europe's most important cities and as a major world power.

After World War II it became the third-largest industrial center in Italy after Milan and Turin. In 1993 it was declared a World Heritage Site by UNESCO, and in 2008 the city hosted the Summer Olympic Games.

The founder of Rome is Romulus who, according to myth, seized the Palatine Hill from its original inhabitants.

He reigned for 43 years after a fabulous life of crime. His successor was Numa Pompilius who established the Roman religion.

In 710 BC the Roman Republic arose under Lucius Tarquinius Priscus who came to power when his father-in-law, King Servius Tullius, was murdered by his wife and her lover.

Priscus established a system of annual magistrates, known as "consuls" and divided Rome into four regions. Priscus was overthrown by Lucius Junius Brutus in 509 BC.

Brutus' son-in-law, Tarquinius Collatinus, became his colleague in 507 BC and the two were deposed by Lucius Junius Brutus in 500 BC when he became sole consul. The Roman Republic was governed by two consuls who alternated their duties each month.

In 494 BC a system of military tribunes with consular powers elected one of theirs number annually as "dictator." The consular tribunes served as judges in important trials and had limited political power. In 443 BC, the office of dictator was established and in 367 BC the office of consul was combined with that of the dictator.

In September 439 BC, a popular uprising led by one Marcus Junius Brutus freed the people from their rule. In 44 BC Julius Caesar deposed Brutus and in 31 BC he became consul and dictator while fighting the civil wars against his political opponent, Mark Antony.

After winning a clear victory against Mark Antony at Philippi he returned to Rome in triumph. He was assassinated on March 15, 44 BC by his close friend Marcus Junius Brutus who had followed him from Gaul into Italy.

From 44-40 BC, Rome was a Republic again. In 40 BC, Octavian (later Augustus) defeated Mark Antony and Cleopatra at the Battle of Actium.

In 27 BC he became Augustus Caesar of Rome and brought the Roman Empire to an end, although it remained an Empire in name only until the rule of Diocletian (284-305 AD).

Augustus reigned for 40 years. He established many political institutions including the Senate, which consisted of 300 men who advised him on legal matters and voted on laws that he proposed.

He also created a system of prefects who ruled Italy along with two consuls who served as judges over civil cases. He also established a standing army which was used to expand Rome's borders. He granted citizenship to all free-born men in the provinces and divided the Empire into provinces each ruled by a governor.

The Pax Romana, or Roman Peace, was the period from 27 BC to 180 AD during which there were no major wars within the Roman Empire. It was during this time that Christianity began to take root within Rome and the rest of Europe.

It was also a time of relative stability within Rome itself as Augustus did not allow public displays of violence and employed an effective police force under Marcus Agrippa. However, there were still slave revolts and frequent uprisings against Roman authority such as in Gaul and Palestine.

However, the stability and prosperity that Augustus brought was not to last. In 5 BC Augustus died and his stepson Tiberius succeeded him as emperor. However, Tiberius had no experience in politics or government so he relied heavily on his friend Sejanus who abused his power.

In AD 26 Sejanus convinced Tiberius to have the Senate acknowledge him as co-Emperor however, he fell from grace when he was arrested and executed shortly afterward for treason. His downfall brought about a brief period of anarchy because Gaius Caesar (Caligula) became Emperor but quickly fell into insanity and was murdered by plotting senators in 41 AD.

The next Emperor, Claudius, was a popular ruler who built many public buildings in Rome and ordered the construction of the first Roman road through Germany. However, in 54 AD he was poisoned and replaced by his wife, Agrippina who held power for six years. Between 55 and 64 AD, there were three different emperors before Nero came to the throne at age 16.

He began his reign promising reforms but soon became tyrannical and corrupt. Finally, he plotted against his mother in 68 AD, had her executed and declared himself "sole ruler and monarch."

In the 70s AD, there were civil wars between supporters of Vespasian who wanted him as Emperor while Otho held power. He was finally defeated by Vespasian's son, Titus, who burned Rome in 79 AD.

The city was sacked and destroyed while the population was slaughtered or sold into slavery. Vespasian returned to Rome as Emperor in 79 AD and rebuilt much of the city. However, there were still uprisings in Gaul as well as a brief rebellion by the governor of Germania.

Nerva became Emperor after Vespasian's death and he lasted for two years before Hadrian came to power in 117 AD. He built the Pantheon, and its circular structure was made of concrete, which became a standard in Roman architecture.

He also built a series of aqueducts. However, his rule was also marked by intrigues among his circle of advisors and constant feuds with the Senate. He was forced to abdicate in 138 AD and was succeeded by Antoninus Pius who reigned for 14 years.

Upon Antoninus Pius' death, an Interregnum (a three-year period without an Emperor) ensued during which there were civil wars for control of Rome from both Parthians and Germanic tribes as well as inter-city warfare among the city's factions.

The final Emperor, Septimus Severius, came to power after Emperor Marcus Aurelius' death in 180 AD. Another Interregnum followed and the Romans encountered a number of Germanic tribes in the 2nd century AD. Between 190 and 285 AD, there were two more interregnums until Diocletian was finally made Emperor by the Praetorian Guard.

Diocletian's reign was marked by increasing military expansion in Africa and consolidation of Roman rule over the city. He enacted changes that allowed him to become godfather of his successor, Maximian, who also took on this role for Diocletian and Constantius I (Constantine) who succeeded him in 305 AD.

Diocletian was the last Emperor to rule over the eastern and western halves of the Empire and he retired in CE 306 AD, handing the power of the eastern half of the Empire to Maximian and Constantius I while Emperor Galerius took the power of Eastern Rome. Diocletian died in CE 312 AD.

During these years, there were also numerous invasions by Germanic tribes from both across the Rhine and Danube rivers.

These included Alamanni, Burgundians, Vandals, Suevi and Franks who often attacked cities or looted them on their way through regions.

Many barbarians were used as garrison troops for various regions in Rome's borders but, eventually, they became a threat themselves. This was partly due to the lack of Roman strength against them and partly because they received constant reinforcements from the Germanic tribes.

This eventually led to a number of bloody battles as the barbarians spread along Rome's borders. In 304 AD, Galerius, the eastern Roman emperor, and Diocletian launched a joint attack against some of his Germanic tribes near Vienna and defeated them (see Battle of Vienna). The response was to move further west with more Germanic tribes such as Huns, Thuringians, Alans and Franks.

In the 4th century, the Huns began to settle in Eastern Europe. Their relations with Rome were mixed and often hostile. One of the Hun leaders, Attila, became famous for his raids against Rome and even sacked the city in 452 AD.

Although the Huns had trouble building their empire with constant warfare with tribes further east such as the Visigoths, they remained a formidable foe for Christianity.

After Attila's death, his kingdom disintegrated fairly quickly and was replaced by smaller states with many different rulers who fought each other for power or looted other territories (see Wars of The Burgundians and wars of The Vandals).

In the chapter "The Tenth Year of Theodoric," Italy is described, referring to a lost number of 10 years (instead of 10 years earlier) in 489 AD.

It says: "In the eighth year of Theodoric, around the end of the year [484/485 AD], Emperor Odoacer and his army crossed the Danube, but nothing is known about it after this. In 488 AD a shamefully low price was offered for their heads and they were deprived of all authority."

It means that at the end of 488 AD, Odoacer's army crossed the Danube and entered the Rhine into Roman Empire. After this point, nothing is known about his army that.

On the other hand, it is not true that Odoacer and his army were deprived of all authority. In fact, Odoacer was appointed Praetorian Prefect (commander of armed forces) and was given the rank of Patrician. After Emperor Anthemius' death on July 11, 472 AD his wife Marcia Euphemia was the de facto ruler while their son Julius Nepos hold the title "imperator" (emperor).

Marcia Euphemia had her son killed and appointed her grandson, Romulus Augustus as Emperor. However, the empire was already on its last legs. It collapsed when Odoacer deposed Emperor Romulus Augustus on September 4, 476, and proclaimed himself King of Italy as King Odovacar.

The Byzantine Empire (sometimes called the Eastern Roman Empire) lasted until 1453 when Constantinople fell to Mehmet II after a siege of 53 days.

However, it had been in decline since the 4th century AD due to invasions by Germanic tribes and Huns while being forced into a war with Persia during which the Persians captured Jerusalem in 614 AD.

The city was retaken in 629 AD by the armies of the Byzantine Emperor Heraclius (who had re-conquered Jerusalem) and then it was lost again to the Persians in 636 AD.

After that time, there were various leaders who tried to reclaim lands in Asia Minor and Anatolia but none of them survived long enough to make any lasting changes. However, in 1071 AD a Turkish commander named Seljuq conquered Baghdad from their Persian conquerors.

He founded the Seljuk Empire which would later be called the Ottoman Empire after his son Suleiman I conquered Constantinople in 1453 CE and brought an end to the Byzantine Empire.

There were many attempts to try to reunite the Roman Empire while the Eastern and Western Empires met in various battles such as the Battle of Adrianople in 378 AD.

However, unity was not achieved and several divisions occurred both within Rome and among its various territories.

The city of Rome has been around for nearly 2,500 years. Before that, it was a small settlement on the Palatine Hill with a population of about 10,000 people. Its status as one of the world's most important historic cities is indisputable.

That said it is still in its infancy when compared to many other world capitals like London and New York City that have largely transformed themselves into modern metropolises since being founded hundreds or even thousands of years ago.

The old districts of Roma are still very much alive but the winding streets and buildings have become all too familiar to tourists as they flock to see ancient ruins or visit attractions while finding somewhere new to eat or stay every day.

Every once in a while, the city acquires a bit of renewed life that is typically followed by developers arriving and changing it for good.

The Romans built beautiful, awe-inspiring buildings all around the city. The ancient Romans had an idea that would eventually lead to what we now know as our modern world and lifestyle. Rome is one of the oldest cities in the world, and it has seen a lot of changes since it was established.

Rome is also the place where you can find some of the most beautiful buildings in the entire world. One of these buildings is The Colosseum. It was built by the Romans in order to host gladiator battles and public spectacles.

This magnificent structure impressed historians and architects all over the world, even today when they see it. The Colosseum can hold up to 55,000 spectators and it is one of those places you cannot help but fall in love with when you visit it. If you want a free tour of the Colosseum, just get yourself a ticket online and join one of the tours.

# Chapter 1: Reasons to Love Rome

If you have the chance, going to Rome is something that you should do.

It is a city with countless reasons why it is worth going to, with new and amazing finds waiting for you everywhere you go.

But if you are still unsure about whether or not you should visit Rome, here are our top reasons why it would be a great idea.

## 1) Rome Has Some of the World's Most Famous Historical Landmarks

When you are visiting Rome, you will see the most famous monuments in the world. If you have a favorite monument (or two), then it would be a great idea to go visit them while you are in the city. Some of these landmarks include The Colosseum, The Pantheon, The Sistine Chapel (the original work is by Michelangelo), and many other famous landmarks.

These make it worth going to Rome because they are must-see attractions for history buffs. By visiting them, you get to see parts of history that are normally off-limits to tourists.

## 2) You Can Experience an Exciting Part of World History While Touring Rome

Rome is one of the most important cities in the area of world history. There are countless reasons why Rome is so important.

It is because of these historical landmarks that it makes it a great place to visit because you can learn more about where you live to people who live in other parts of the world.

## 3) You Will Get to Experience Some Fantastic Food While You Are in Rome

If you are a foodie at heart, then going to Rome will be your best choice for foodies around the world. In this city, you can't go more than a few feet without stumbling on a food specialty.

There are numerous pasta dishes, pizza, gelato (ice cream), and of course, there is the legendary Italian cuisine that has made its way around the world.

## 4) You Will Have the Opportunity to See Some Rare and Exotic Animals While Touring Rome

If you love animals (who doesn't?), then here is another reason why going to Rome would make for a great experience for you. There are a number of different animals that you can see while you are in this city.

You can see parrots, storks, dolphins and many more animals that are strictly limited to Rome. With the abundance of these animals, it is clear that Rome is a place with plenty of wealth.

## 5) You Will Have the Chance to Explore Beautiful Ruins

Many people know about the city of Pompeii and Herculaneum, but few know about the city of Ostia Antica. These ruins are located approximately 45 minutes outside Rome, and they are quite breathtaking when you see them up close.

These ruins are what people would have seen when they were going into and out of Rome. These ruins are considered to be the earliest Roman ruins and are definitely worth seeing.

## 6) There Are Some Wild, Exciting, and Amazing Things to See While You Are Here

There is an abundance of different things to see in Rome. If you really want to see what it is all about, then going on a tour would be the best choice for you.

However, as long as you don't go on one of those cheesy "tourist trap" pilgrimages, then any tour should be fine when you visit Rome in person. There is plenty of fun to have when you visit this city due to its impressive history and culture.

## 7) You Will Have the Chance to Meet Some of the World's Greatest Artists While in Rome

When you travel on your trip, you usually find yourself meeting some people from places that you have never been to before. But when you travel to Rome, this will not be a problem. Since Rome is one of the most important cities in the world, there are many different artists in this city who are famous for their work around the world. Not only can you meet these artists, but they probably still live here too!

## 8) You Will Have a Great Sense of History and Tradition While Touring This City

Rome is full of history and tradition due to being from such an important city in our past. There are many different things that you can do in this city to give you a true sense of these two important factors. Whether it is going out to a historical site, taking a trip to the Vatican (the home of one of the most famous artists in history), or just walking around Rome, you will be able to get a taste of what life was like for the ancient Romans.

## 9) There Are So Many Different Ways that You Can Travel While in Rome

If you are looking for an exciting trip during your summer break, then going to Rome is definitely an excellent choice. There are endless possibilities when it comes to venturing around this city. You can walk, take the bus, take a tour, or just find your own way. There are various stops you can make on your trip to Rome that will help you get around this incredible city.

## 10) Going to Rome Will Provide You with an Unforgettable Experience

Rome is one of the most exciting places to visit not only because of its rich history and culture but also due to its amazing nature. This city is filled with excitement due to being one of the most important cities in history.

Rome will provide you with so many different ways that you can have fun while you are there. With all of this going for it, you can see why Rome is a great choice for your upcoming trip!

So there you have it. You now know some of the awesome reasons why going to Rome would be a great choice for your summer vacation! With the abundance of amazing things that this city has to offer, there is no doubt that many people are eager to come travel here.

Paul Tryon argues that Rome is primarily responsible for the development of Western civilization. He believes that "Rome furnished the model which has remained in force in modern Western culture" because it was a city that flourished while other cities were destroyed. Because of this, Romans became a symbol in Western culture.

The Roman Empire began to fall apart around 400 AD and by 600 AD it was no longer a united empire. Rome's great architectural legacy continues today. Its architectural legacy is visible throughout all of Europe and even some parts of Asia Minor (now Turkey).

A simple stroll down any street or sidewalk will tell you just how much Roman architecture was present all throughout the Empire from its founding until its fall.

The Roman Pantheon (also known as the Imperial Basilica of the Pantheon) is the best-preserved and most recognizable building from the era. The main part of this building was built in 27 BC and has withstood several earthquakes. This building can be found on either end of the Piazza Venezia near and around the Trajan's Forum.

Many contributions to architecture are found in Rome today, including architectural styles in churches, basilicas and forums like Pompeii's forum, Colosseum and Trajan's Forum. Some buildings were built for specific reasons or to hold a specific item such as a treasure, temple or statue.

# Chapter 2: Best Time to Visit

There are many arguments for and against when is the best time to visit Rome. Depending on who you ask, the correct answer might be completely different. This attempts to cover these valid points of view and provide a helpful overview of what you can expect when visiting Rome during specific seasons, times of day, and holidays.

For example, if you're interested in experiencing a city at its most lively during the daytime hours, traveling between would be optimal. If your interest is in capturing breathtaking scenes at night while avoiding the 9 am and 1 pm crowds that emerge as daylight fades away, then visiting between 3 pm and 6 pm would be ideal. And of course, if you're interested in enjoying extensive shopping during the day and visiting ruins at night, then traveling between 9 am and 3 pm would be ideal.

Just as the hours of daylight change throughout the year, so does the time period when Rome's best attractions are opened to visitors. During peak seasons, crowds can be heavy and often line up long before opening. To avoid this, consider visiting during off-peak times like late mornings or early evenings while Rome has a lighter crowd. If you're not sure of which days those are, simply ask at any tourist information booth located around Rome.

In addition, you may want to consider avoiding long lines by visiting popular attractions in the early morning. While this is not possible for many of the Roman Colosseum or Vatican Museums, you can easily visit the Trevi Fountain well before peak hours begin. You can also avoid long lines at the Pantheon, Spanish Steps, and various Roman museums much more easily than many of Rome's major attractions.

When it comes to crowds and tourist attractions, it's important not to limit yourself to specific neighborhoods during your trip. Rome is full of impressive ruins located in different areas throughout town. Some of Rome's major landmarks are located within the city center, including the Colosseum, St. Peter's Basilica, Roman Forum, and the Vatican Museums. Other impressive ruins are located just outside the city center along Rome's metro line. Among these are the Pantheon, Spanish Steps, Trevi Fountain, and Porta Pia.

No matter when you decide to arrive in Rome or for how long you plan to stay there, there is something for every type of traveler to see and do throughout the year. You might catch a glimpse of Pope Francis while visiting St. Peter's Square or try your hand at shopping at a seasonal outdoor fair during your trip to Italy. No matter what your interests are, there are many rewarding experiences awaiting you during your time in Rome.

The busiest time to visit Rome is spring and autumn, the reason for this is that during the summer most of the city wants to avoid the high temperatures, so people escape to the coast and most events happen in either spring or autumn.

August is the worst time to visit because it's hot and crowded with tourists, plus much of the city is closed as the locals are on vacation. Many Italians take the entire of August and go on vacation. Italian weather has a typical Mediterranean climate which means the city has a hot and muggy summer.

The temperatures start to rise in May, though they never really get freezing, even in winter. From October through April, many attractions operate on a shorter-hour schedule, and some choose to renovate at this time.

From November through February, the beachfront area is deserted, and it can get a little colder by the sea. Rome doesn't get a lot of rainfall no matter what time of year it is, and this can help the humidity a little even when the temperatures frequently rise above 30°C in summer.

## Spring

March can be slightly chilly in the evenings still, and with temperatures still in the 50s, it's a good idea to bring a jacket. March sees the Rome Marathon bring plenty of visitors into the city but other than the main sights, things may be open. Many attractions still operate winter hours until at least April, so it's essential to check hours and times until the end of April.

Holy Week and Easter in April also mean that you can expect closures at religious sights and more observances. May is a great shoulder month to visit because the weather has warm temperatures, which can get as high as the mid-70s.

The hotels start to increase their prices, but it's less likely to book up as far in advance as June. The International Horse Show and the International Literature festival both take place in spring and bring a small influx of visitors.

## Summer

This is the busiest tourist season, and the city is packed with tourists. June through August is the busiest since the weather is in the high 80's and the high temperatures high prices. September still has suitable temperatures, but lines tend to be much smaller, especially at the most prominent attractions. The prices are still high through September, and you can see events like the Festa di Noantri and the White Night of Rome.

## Autumn

October through November sees rates fall sharply, and temperatures resemble spring. October sees many stores start changing to winter hours, and by November, you should check hours and opening times for any activities. You can still find several large festivals at this time and Opera season is undoubtedly popular in Rome, and this is the best time to go for music lovers.

## Winter

Rome gets cold in winter, with temperatures dropping into the 30s.

## Tips When Visiting Rome

If you're planning a trip to Italy, then the best time to visit is in the spring or summer. The weather is milder and it will be easier to navigate around the city. That being said, there are some things you should do before you go—like book your flights and hotels—and these tips can help you avoid any difficulties with transportation or finding places to stay while in town:

- Book your flights as early as possible because they cost less the closer it gets to your travel date. You'll also have more options for when you want to travel.

- Book your accommodation six months in advance. Many hotels and Roman apartments get booked quickly, so if you don't get the spot you want, you could end up paying more than usual or have to wait until they free up. If you're visiting during Easter, book early because there will be many more people from all over the world in town.

- If you're visiting during a special event or festival like the Roman Easter celebrations, avoid booking around those dates because it will be particularly crowded and expensive because there are many tourists in town.

- Find out the public transportation system and sites you want to see beforehand. Rome is not easy to navigate, especially if you don't speak Italian.

- If you're traveling with children, try to avoid school holidays because most of the schools will be closed during those times so it will be less crowded.

- Consider traveling the week between Christmas or New Year's Day and the Epiphany on January 6th because the Romans take a break from work that week (and they party) and many of them don't return back to work until after January 6th.

- If you plan on taking a cooking class at Città del Gusto, avoid Sundays because that's the only day they don't offer classes.

- Arrive early and take the Metro directly to the Colosseum because you can avoid long lines. Otherwise, arrive as early as you can and try to avoid going on weekdays when it is raining or cold.

- Take a good camera with you and, if you have a smartphone, download an offline map app like Google Map for Rome so you'll be able to navigate around town without worrying about using up your data or having poor reception in some places.

- Pack as lightly as you can. You'll be traveling on a train and walking among crowds all day, so you don't want to carry anything that you won't need.

- Bring extra cash since there are very few ATMs in Rome, so they will charge you a fee for using one.

- Stay outside the center of Rome because it's a lot easier to navigate around the city when you're not inside the Pantheon or Piazza Navona.

- Leave your valuables in your hotel safe or lock them safely in your suitcase. In addition, when you travel to Italy, especially in Europe, you shouldn't use ATMs since they can be difficult to access.

- Car rentals are plentiful and inexpensive in Italy. They will also take care of the breakdown service as well, so if your car breaks down or runs out of gas on the way to Rome, you won't need to deal with it yourself.

- Leave behind any backpacks or heavy luggage because there are frequent pick pocketings and bag snatchers around tourist attractions.

- Don't wear bulky clothing because then it could hinder your movement while walking or sitting.

- Avoid wearing expensive jewelry like watches, necklaces or bracelets, because they may be stolen.

- As a precautionary measure, carry your passport in a different, inconspicuous place than your cash wallet so that the pick pockets won't steal the wallet and access the rest of your money.

- Watch out for thieves around tourist attractions and look around when you're sitting down in cafes or restaurants. Ask for a "check please" or give them your credit card to pay rather than handing over the card directly to them so they can't take it with them if they manage to get away with something else.

- Be careful when you cross the street since cars are allowed to park on the sidewalks and they may not be paying attention to pedestrian traffic.

- Always be aware of your surroundings, especially at night, because there may be pick pockets or thieves lurking about.

- Always carry ample amounts of cash. ATMs are scarce, so it is easier to exchange US dollars for Euros instead of carrying around a lot of US dollars with you.

- Always use a credit card when shopping, even if you're paying cash for a meal or in a bar. If you don't, the shopkeepers may charge your credit card without your permission.

- Try to eat at restaurants that are outside of the city center where it'll be cheaper and less crowded. Stay away from restaurants with special offers and deals since they are usually more expensive than other restaurants in the area. In addition, try not to eat near tourist attractions because they will charge you more than you should have paid.

- Avoid using public transportation on weekdays because it's crowded.

- Don't just follow people around, especially if they are in a group and you don't know them. If people seem suspicious or are trying to strike up a conversation with you, always avoid them.

- Try to travel during the day when it won't rain since it may be uncomfortable walking through wet streets or stumbling on the uneven pavement in the rain.

- Be careful when buying souvenirs because they will often be counterfeit or of poor quality.

- Be careful with your money in general. If you're using cash, be sure to always tuck it away securely in your wallet or pocket. Wear a money belt with the cash for extra protection.

- Always use a money belt or secure it under your clothing unless you want to wear a bulky jacket that may not be very comfortable and inhibit your movement.

- Don't wear expensive jewelry like watches, necklaces or bracelets because they are easily stolen and may lead you to be robbed on the street if you don't lock them away securely.

- Don't carry any valuables in your pockets. Carry a camera around your neck with the shutter button on the cord to prevent it from getting lost or stolen.

- Watch out for people standing on sidewalks trying to distract you when crossing the street so that they can pick your pocket, and don't wear pants with large back pockets since they could easily be taken advantage of when you're not paying attention.

- Never leave valuables and expensive items in plain view in your hotel room like cameras and laptops since they could easily be stolen.

- Stand away from the front door when using your cell phone since thieves could easily snatch it out of your hand or pocket if you're not paying attention.

# Chapter 3: Rome's Must-See Attractions

Rome is full of beautiful sights, historical sites, and hidden treasures. There's no better way to get your bearings in the Eternal City than by exploring one of its top 20 must-see attractions. From Colosseum to Pantheon, Vatican City to Vittorio Emanuele II Monument, these are the places you simply have to visit while in Italy's largest city.

If you're ever planning a trip or need some inspiration for what things to see first when visiting Rome, then this is for you! We've listed our favorite 20 sites that will give you a true taste of what makes this city unique. Only one of these attractions is covered in detail below, the rest are all listed in paragraph form along with where they're located, and a short description.

It's worth noting that this list is purely based on our own opinions. If you disagree with any of our choices then please let us know! We want to provide you with the best travel tips we possibly can before you visit Rome so that your trip is as enjoyable as possible.

# 1. Colosseum

Address: Via delle Terme di Tito, Roma

The Colosseum is perhaps the most famous attraction in Rome and one of the best tourist traps in the world. It's impossible to deny how beautiful and majestic this building is. However, it's hard to ignore that the only real purpose behind this monstrous edifice was to host gladiatorial combat between humans and animals. That being said, it's still astonishing how a massive amphitheater could be built (with slave labor) by just 2,000 people in just 10 years!

To even begin to understand why this place matters you need to know some history. The Colosseum was originally built as a venue for spectator games by the Caesars. The story of its construction is akin to something out of Game of Thrones. There were two architects in charge of the project, one working on the foundations and the other on the walls. The former was considerably slower due to his old age so he would regularly send his son ahead to give updates to his father "in order for him not be ashamed" and keep up with the faster-working younger man. Eventually, this resulted in both men being executed when it became apparent that they had failed to meet their target deadline. The Colosseum eventually served its purpose and was never dismantled or occupied again. Until the mid-19th century, it was still being used for public spectacles, including mock battles between actors wearing helmets and armor!

The Colosseum is located in the southern part of Rome known as 'Trastevere'. The city's main train station (Roma Termini) is located close by so you can come here on foot. If you don't have time to visit all 20 attractions on this list then we recommend at least stopping off at this one. From there, you can head to the Roman Forum and Palatine Hill.

## 2. Forum Romanum

Address: Via dei Fori Imperiali, Roma

As is suggested by the name, the Forum Romanum was built as a series of large decorative squares flanked by important monuments like temples and basilicas. It was also where ancient Rome's political life was centered on with legal matters being discussed in the Basilica Julia. There are several ancient structures still standing here including Trajan's Column, the Temple of Antoninus and Faustina, and The Altar of Peace. These buildings are exquisite examples of ancient Roman architecture so it's worth bringing your camera. Unlike the Colosseum, you won't be able to walk around this site as many of the ruins have been covered for safety reasons.

Forum Romanum is located in a busy part of central Rome near Piazza Venezia. There's not much to see here so it's better to just stop off for 15 minutes at most. You can also visit the nearby Capitoline Hill while you're in the area. To get here, go to Stazione Termini then follow Via del Corso until you reach Piazza Venezia.

## 3. St. Peter's Basilica

Address: Piazza San Pietro, Roma

Located just across the road from Vatican City is the massive St. Peter's Basilica. It was built by Pope Julius II and is part of the complex of buildings that make up Vatican City. You'll need to book ahead if you want to get a spot inside for one of their free guided tours which are offered between 10 am and 3 pm every day except Sundays and public holidays. When we visited it was incredibly busy inside with a small waiting time for security checks so we didn't bother going in this time. You can still view the interior of the church from a distance as it's right on top of a grand Roman landmark.

The St. Peter's Basilica is in the center of Rome near Viale Vaticano, just off of Via del Corso.

## 4. Piazza Navona and Campo de' Fiori

There are several important monuments in this plaza which are worth checking out whether you're staying near them or not. It was once the main marketplace for the city so you'll see lots of souvenir shops selling various fake artwork and polished marble statuettes.

## 5. Piazza del Popolo

This is one of the main parks in Rome and is prominent due to its location at the top of a hill. There is a lot of artwork and statues hanging in the park including the iconic "Pieta." If you're staying near this area you can pop on down to check it out then do some wandering around before heading back up to your hotel for lunch and dinner.

## 6. Pantheon

Pantheon was built to serve as a temple dedicated to all Roman gods but when Constantine converted Rome from paganism into Christianity it became a Christian church instead.

Today it is the main and most famous church in Rome and is well worth visiting at least once if you are short on time. The inside of the Pantheon is gorgeous and there are lots of statues lining the inside as well as gorgeous fresco paintings.

## 7. Trevi Fountain

The Trevi Fountain is another popular tourist spot in Rome located right over the main entrance to the city called Piazza di Spagna.

This fountain was built by Bernini in 1732 as a monument to his patron, Pope Clement XII. You can see Bernini's trademark use of curved lines throughout the structure including the arches of doorways and some of the stonework on pedestals and columns.

Lastly, I stood under the dome, relishing the quiet, peaceful and magical space. Check out my photos.

The interior of St. Peter's Basilica is truly a sight like no other; at least that's what I heard. I know you're probably thinking it's just another church but throw in the fact that this church is more than sacred to Catholics everywhere and is said to be the burial site of Saint Peter and you'll have an idea of what it feels like to stand in this holy place.

Albeit a day trip because of traffic along Via Nazionale (a short 5-minute drive from our farmhouse), I found myself at St. Peter's Basilica earlier today.

This 500-year old church sits on the side of a hill, overlooking some of the most famous sights in Rome: Trevi Fountain and Piazza di Spagna.

The church takes up a lot of real states because it is built not only to fit the land but it's also built at an angle with its highest point resting on the ground.

If you've ever been to St. Peter's Square in front of this church then you will know what I'm talking about when I say that you can walk all around and view every part of this magnificent structure without ever having to climb stairs or ascend any staircases.

The inside of the church is built for grandeur. What stands out to me is how everything is so ornate, nothing quite fits together, and it just looks like it's all in a rush to finish before someone on the outside decides to come in and start tearing up all the scaffolding, exposing all its imperfections. If it weren't for Saint Peter's Basilica then I would go as far as to say that this may be one of my favorite churches in Rome. It isn't necessarily better than other churches in Rome, but because of its absolute dominance as a structure on top of a hill overlooking the Trevi Fountain and Piazza di Spagna—it just feels more important than others.

## 8. Piazza del Popolo

Address: Fontana delle Naiadi, Piazza del Popolo, Roma

Piazza del Popolo is a large rectangular square with some famous Roman landmarks such as the Barcaccia Fountain and the Obelisk of Montecitorio. It's a great place to hang out and enjoy the sunshine, have a meal, or pick up some souvenirs on your way to another destination.

The square is located in the center of Rome near Piazza di Spagna. If you want to visit Piazza del Popolo then there are plenty of ways to get here as it's quite central in Rome. You could walk from many different places including the Colosseum, or take a taxi from anywhere else for €10-€20 depending on traffic. It's best to go early in the morning if you don't want to fight through crowds of tourists or have any things stolen by pickpockets while you're perusing the shops here. The stores can get pretty crowded.

## 9. Palazzo della Civiltà Italiana

Address: Largo della Civilita Italiana, Roma

The Palazzo della Civiltà Italiana was built by architect Marcello Piacentini to represent the major achievements of centuries of Italian history and culture. It is definitely worth a quick stop on your travels around Rome as there is a lot to see here in a small space. One of the main highlights at this site is the giant mural which illustrates the various stages of human progress throughout history. It was painted in the 1960s by artist Amedeo Modigliani.

The Palazzo della Civiltà Italiana is located on Via Nazionale in a central part of Rome. It's not somewhere that you want to miss if you're staying within walking distance which is at least a 5-minute walk from the Farmshop Albergaria Trastevere. Alternatively, you can take a taxi from any other spot for €10-€20 depending on traffic; it's best to book ahead as the lineups can get pretty long on weekends and public holidays.

## 10. Roman Forum

Address: Piazza Venezia, Roma.

The Roman Forum is a large rectangular square located close to the Colosseum. The people who lived in ancient Rome considered this huge square to be one of the most important areas of the city due to all of the important buildings that surround it.

There's a pair of buildings called the Arch of Septimius Severus and the Arch of Constantine that you can check out which were built by these prominent Romans.

## 11. Piazza Navona

Address: Piazza Navona, Roma

The Piazza Navona is one of many gorgeous squares that flank roads throughout Rome. On the south side of this square is one of Rome's most famous fountains, the Fontana dei Quattro Fiumi.

If you had to pick one square in all of Rome to visit then I would recommend this one because it just has so much character. There are several grand buildings like the Palazzo della Cancelleria, Palazzo Pamphili, and Palazzo Doria Pamphilj standing here which make for some great photo opportunities.

The Piazza Navona is located near Campo de' Fiori and is a popular spot for picking up souvenirs in Rome. The square is also just off Piazza Venezia, one of the main squares in Rome.

## 12. Campo de' Fiori

Address: Campo de' Fiori, Roma

Campo de' Fiori is a small square located in the center of Rome near Piazza Navona and Piazza del Popolo. Many Roman locals come here during the daytime to have a bite to eat or to sit outside and socialize with friends over coffee or drinks. It's also famous for its fruit stand which sells all sorts of exotic fruits from around the world. It's quite popular with tourists so you'll see lots of fashion stores selling cheap knock-off clothing and bags.

## 13. Galleria Borghese

Address: Via IV-VII Settembre, Roma 00187

The Galleria Borghese is a great art museum located in central Rome. It was built over 140 years ago by an aristocrat who wanted to create a gallery that displayed the best art pieces in Italy. It now has one of the largest private art collections in the world with over 8,000 masterpieces including paintings, sculptures, drawings, prints, and other works of art by both famous artists and up-and-coming artists too. It's a great place to visit whether you're a fan of art or not but I must warn you, there is a lot of foot traffic and you'll need to take some time finding your way around the museum if you're unfamiliar with it. It's not easy to get lost in this place and around the back, there are some amazing pieces including Raphael's "The School of Athens."

The Galleria Borghese sits on Piazza del Popolo in central Rome; it's a short walk from our farmhouse just over a 2-minute walk from Via del Corso. There are many ways to get here so check Google maps for directions.

## 14. Piazza di Spagna

Address: Piazza di Spagna, Roma

Piazza di Spagna is a main square in Rome located close to a famous monument that you shouldn't miss out on seeing while you're here. If you travel on foot from the Colosseum then it will only take about 20 minutes to arrive at Piazza di Spagna. The square is named after the Spanish Embassy and was called "Spanish Steps" when it was built in 1725. People who live in Rome say that this is one of their favorite places because there are always beautiful people standing around to watch and tourists coming from all over the world to enjoy entrances, cafes, and restaurants.

## 15. Piazza del Popolo

Address: Piazza del Popolo, Roma

Piazza del Popolo is the main square in Rome located near the Spanish Steps and just behind the Vatican Museum. The most famous landmark in this square is the large Egyptian obelisk standing tall in the center which was first built by a pharaoh for Queen Hatshepsut back in 1450 BC. There are lots of cafes around here which will play background music that you can enjoy while you people watch for a bit.

# Chapter 4: Beyond the Center: Unusual Things to Do in Rome

While Rome is undoubtedly one of the world's most famous cities, it also offers plenty for the more curious tourist to explore. In this, we present an assortment of things to do in Rome that you'd be unlikely to find in any other city. Beyond the Center looks at a few oddities that have earned the city its reputation as something not quite like anywhere else.

## Clothing Optional Beaches

Cities around the world have their own beach culture, but you'll never get to experience that in Rome. The city is not located on a coastline, and the water quality is too poor for swimming anyway.

So why are there signs advertising beaches that are clothing optional? These places may be beaches, but they're not what you'd expect. They are chaste-sounding "naturist" establishments where clothing is optional (usually only worn by staff) and the holiday involves barbecues, sunbathing and watersports without ever getting into a swimsuit. The most famous is Bagno Erotici, located in the Parco degli Acquedotti, but there are plenty of others to choose from.

## Michelangelo's House and a Tour of All His Works in the City

If you're interested in art and architecture, you could visit the city for months on end and not see everything Michelangelo has contributed to Rome. His works can be seen all over the city but it takes an expert eye to find them — he also lived here for many years at a time. His house can be found in what is now known as Via del Corso after moving out of Trastevere back in 1550. It's not open to the public, but a tour through the streets takes in his greatest works including San Pietro in Vincoli and the façade of Santa Maria Sopra Minerva.

## Quirky Museum Openings

You probably know that Rome's museums are free — but did you know some of them have openings with a difference? In recent years, many institutions have begun opening their doors, especially to children. Kids can take part in arts and crafts sessions, storytelling and workshops with their favorite characters at times when adults are feeling excluded from the art world. The MAXXI art gallery in the EUR has regular workshops for kids with popular cartoon characters, and the Palazzo Massimo hosts children's films on opening nights.

## Theatre Festivals

Rome is an international city so it comes as no surprise that it hosts a range of theatre festivals throughout the year. Most involve Italian acts though there are some exceptions including late-night performances from French, Spanish and German troupes, which can be found from June to September. During the other seasons, you can enjoy everything from tango theatre to puppet shows at the Teatro dell' Orologio. Theatre troupes from other countries also put on performances demonstrating the cultural diversity and richness that makes Rome so unique.

## Nocturnal Flights in a Hot Air Balloon

This one is a little more extravagant but it's not impossible to find in Rome. The city's Grand Roman Hotel has taken advantage of its immediate proximity to Fiumicino airport and built an open-air heliport with landing lights to allow guests direct access to the sky for hot air balloon flights which can be enjoyed at night for an extra romantic touch. There are also gondola rides on the hotel's rooftop in the summer.

## Hidden Beer Garden at the German Embassy

Not many people realize that Rome has a German embassy, but it does and, more unusually, it has a beer garden. The 15th-century Villa Spada houses the embassy and the beer garden is located next to the villa's magnificent park which can be accessed on Sundays when the garden is open to the public. It's an oasis of peace in a city filled with noise and traffic. You can even enjoy your drink on one of Germany's famous wooden benches.

## Drinking at a Fountain

We're not talking about a trip to the Trevi Fountain — any tourist can do that. The city's many fountains are everywhere, so grab your bottle of wine or grappa and get drinking. It's perfectly legal to drink at a fountain (though only the ones without statues) as long as you have a container, but it's probably best to avoid monuments such as Piazza Navona where police are more likely to intervene. Head somewhere like the vast gardens surrounding Termini station if you want peace and quiet. Another quirky option is the fountain at the bottom of Tre Scalini in Trastevere — it's a favorite with Romans.

## Pizza from a Hotplate

If you've never tried street food, this is your chance to fill up on a classic Roman treat. A hotplate pizza restaurant has a power source installed outside where pizzas are cooked in front of the customer, but you can also order al taglio from inside if you want some privacy. The best thing about this particular foodie trend is that it's relatively cheap — a Margherita costs less than €3 and there are plenty of arancini to go around too.

## Gelato in a Bath

In summer, a trip to the Lido di Ostia Antica is not just for sunbathing and swimming. The park's fountain and an ice-cream stall have also been installed. You can sit and soak up the atmosphere while enjoying any one of hundreds of flavors of sorbetto, the gelato's Italian cousin.

# Food on Film at Rome's Open Air Cinema Festival

For a truly classic experience, head to the open-air cinema festival in August at Piazza Navona. It features countless videos from all over Italy accompanied by live music.

## Theatre with a View

Rome's world-famous opera house, Teatro dell'Opera, is the ideal place for a romantic evening. The theatre is not just famous for its opera productions—it also hosts everything from concerts to ballet. It also has a café downstairs where you can enjoy an interval drink while admiring the amazing architecture and stunning frescos.

## Love on the Bridge at Villa Sciarra

Get your creative juices flowing and write your own love story on Rome's iconic Ponte Milvio bridge with candles, sweets or cards that you can leave as clues to help find your love. There are several places to do this, but Piazza Leonardo da Vinci is particularly romantic.

## Epicurean Roof-Top Feast at the Hotel D'Italia

Enjoy your city break on the roof terrace of Rome's most luxurious hotel and participate in a culinary feast with a view. This event has taken place every summer since 2012 and is well worth checking out if you're interested in new food trends.

# Romantic Package with Aperitivo

Aperitivo is a time-honored tradition in Italy. The word 'aperitivo' actually means 'before dinner.' We recommend the Hotel Palmaiola where you can enjoy an aperitif on the rooftop terrace overlooking the city. It also has a pool and hot tub perfect for relaxing after your romantic date in Rome. View hotel deals here.

Rome's most romantic restaurant — Antica Hosteria — is located at the bottom of the Spanish Steps and is known for great food, huge portions and reasonable prices. Book your table here: www.anticahosteriaonline.com/en .htm

# The Fountain of the Four Rivers

Located in the center of Piazza Navona, this 19$^{th}$-century fountain, by Gian Lorenzo Bernini depicts four male figures representing the four main rivers that are most important to ancient Rome: the Nile, Ganges, Danube and Plate. The four female figures symbolizing Earth are meant to protect them from above. This fountain is a true masterpiece and a popular meeting place for locals and tourists alike.

# The Portico d'Ottavia at Largo di Torre Argentina

This portico was built in honor of Octavia, sister of Caesar Augustus. She was also the wife of Mark Antony, one of the great leaders of the Roman Empire.

# The Fountain of Apollodorus

Named after its sculptor, this is one of the best-preserved ancient fountains in Rome. It dates back to 19 BC and its main feature is a statue representing Hercules standing over a man sitting on a giant turtle.

## The Garden of Villa Medici

Located at Piazza di Spagna (Spanish Square), this garden houses some works by famous modern artists such as Alberto Giacometti and Salvador Dali as well as ancient Roman sculptures

## Piazza del Popolo

This is one of Rome's largest squares and the second largest in Rome after Piazza di Spagna. It may also well be the city's most beautiful square and one of its most famous.

## The Spanish Steps

The Piazza di Spagna is located at the foot of the Spanish Steps, which were made famous by the movie 'Three Coins in a Fountain' with Audrey Hepburn.

## Castel Sant'Angelo

Castel Sant'Angelo was built as a mausoleum for Emperor Hadrian. The fortress-like structure is located on the Tiber River in Vatican City.

## Palazzo Laterano

The Palazzo Laterano is located on the east end of the Via del Corso, near Via Veneto and is considered one of Rome's finest Renaissance buildings. The Palazzo belonged to a famous family of popes, the Barberini and was built between 1474 and 1563.

## Piazza Venezia

A must-visit in Rome for lovers, this piazza is located at a crossing of three important streets: Via del Teatro di Marcello, Via del Corso and Via dei Condotti. The most famous landmark in the area is the magnificent Victor Emanuel Monument.

## Sant'Ignazio Church

This is the ideal place to visit on a date or for your wedding. The church was commissioned by Pope Clement XIII and specially designed to accommodate pilgrims from Piedmont and Liguria who were visiting Rome at that time. In 1773, a peace treaty between Spain and Portugal was signed in Sant'Ignazio Church and, later in 1816, it was where the body of Napoleon was kept before burial.

## San Lorenzo Maggiore

One of Rome's biggest churches, San Lorenzo Maggiore was built between 1577 and 1754. The façade is a masterpiece by Bernini and the inside is richly decorated with paintings by Raphael and Caravaggio. It's also worth seeing the fountain in front of the church because it has changed so many times over the years. At present, it shows Baroque, Neo-classical and Romantic statues.

## Piazza Navona

Located near the Pantheon, Piazza Navona is one of Rome's most beautiful piazzas. It was built over what was once a lake. The best-known feature of the piazza is the Fontana dei Quattro Fiumi, which was built in 1651. This is an example of Bernini's well-known baroque style.

## The Colonne di San Pietro

These four colossal columns originally stood in front of St Peter's Basilica. They were removed in the 18th century and today they are located at the Piazza Colonna, where they form one of Rome's most famous monuments.

The columns are made of granite and are approximately 4m high. The four faces of the column form a cross — one for each century.

## Trajan's Markets

These are some of the most ancient markets in Rome. Trajan's Markets were part of the first imperial forum built by Emperor Trajan, beginning in 113 AD and they ran from 100-115 AD.

Today, the markets are still run according to the original system — there is an auctioneer who shouts out prices and then people walk up to him or her to buy items or sell their own goods.

## The Riverbank

The Tiber flows through the city center and upon it you can see the most magnificent monuments of Rome. There are two bridges: the Ponte Cestio connects Centro Storico and Trastevere to each other, while the Ponte Sant'Angelo was built by Pope Leo I in the 6th century to gain access to the Castrum Patrium (the stronghold of Pope Nicholas III), which was located nearby.

## Trajan's Forum

Trajan's Forum is a large architectural complex on Via dei Fori Imperiali that was built by Emperor Trajan between 113 and 117 AD. This is where you will find Trajan's Column—a masterpiece by Apollodorus of Damascus that is 23 m high and decorated with scenes of the imperial army's victory over the Dacians in 101-102 AD.

## The Cappella Arcivescovile

This chapel is located near St Peter's Basilica in Vatican City and was constructed between 1568 and 1571 as a mausoleum for Cardinal Melchior de Polignac by Giacomo della Porta. The chapel is particularly popular because it houses some of the most beautiful paintings from the 16th century, including works by Caravaggio, Raphael and Titian.

## The Pantheon

The Pantheon was built in 27 BC and expanded in 121 AD. It is a circular building that also serves as a church. The edifice has become an architectural icon of Rome due to its massive two-tiered portico—one of the largest ever conceived by ancient Roman architects.

## Palatine Hill

This hill adopts the shape of a horseshoe and is located behind the Colosseum, which is why it bears its name 'Pantheon' ('Great Altar'). The hill was inhabited in ancient times by many centurions—young Roman soldiers who served under the command of their centurion.

## Colosseum

The Colosseum was built between 72 and 81 AD by Emperor Vespasian. It used to be the largest in the world and can now only be called a shadow of its former self. However, it still remains one of Rome's most popular tourist attractions and is open to visitors year-round. The Colosseum is also home to many dramatic shows and concerts, such as 'Roman Summer Nights' which takes place in August each year.

## St Peter's Basilica

St Peter's Basilica is one of the most impressive churches in Rome. Located on Piazza San Pietro, it is also the largest church in the world. The first three Popes who ruled over the church were buried in this basilica (Peter, Linus, and Cletus). This is also where you can find Michelangelo's Pietà, a marble sculpture that depicts the body of Jesus after his crucifixion.

## Santa Maria in Trastevere

This church was built around the middle of the 6th century and is the best example of ancient Roman architecture in Rome. It was originally a pagan temple dedicated to what the Italians call 'Fortuna Primigenia' (the primordial goddess of fortune) and is also known as 'Santa Maria Maggiore' (the greater church).

## Piazza della Repubblica

This square is located right in front of Palazzo Chigi, which houses two ministries: Foreign Affairs and Interior. The square has undergone a real makeover since it became trendy among celebrities and fashionistas.

# Chapter 5: Eating in Rome

Eating in Rome, Italy is an experience unlike any other. With over a million tourists hopping on trains and by car every day, the Italian capital's culinary scene is frenetic with energy and excitement.

It's hard to pick a favorite spot here because the food options are all around you at all times—you can grab a quick bite across from your hotel or dine down at one of the Michelin-starred restaurants in your pocket. No matter where you're staying or what time of day it is, there will be plenty of places to find something to eat that will make you feel like royalty as long as you have some Italian cash (and not too much else).

# Breakfast

La Corriera (Via Fosso di San Gregorio, 9) is a perfect spot for a morning meal. The food will jumpstart your Italian vocabulary as you try to order some of the most basic dishes — mamaliga (cornmeal mush), sunny-side-up eggs, omelets, and freshly squeezed orange juice. The coffee is not bad either; it's strong and aromatic. When you sit at the outside tables here, the neighborhood locals will start to interact with you as they pass by. You'll feel like one of them when you finish your meal here.

S'Eat (Via Capo d'Africa, 2) is a great option for breakfast if you're craving eggs and traditional Italian fare. Their grande panino (sandwich) options are a little pricey, but the quality is extremely good.

La Bottega del Vino (Via dell'Acquedotto, 6) is the perfect place to try some authentic Roman cuisine at night — something that's not so different from what one would expect to find in Tuscany or Umbria. La Bottega will also provide you with some of the best local wines (and beer and moonshine) to go with your meal.

# Lunch/Dinner

Carlo DeMarco (Via dei Reti 9) serves up excellent wood-oven pizza, pasta, and seafood dishes in a modern yet comfortable atmosphere. Don't expect anything spectacular here, but you will be treated well if you're in Rome. The only warning here is that they sell out quickly — which is most likely due to the fact that it's just so darn good!

La Mela Vecchia (Piazza di Santo Stefano 6) is a great spot for dinner. It is a casual restaurant located right in the heart of the city's historical center. If you're a vegetarian, this place has one of the best pasta dishes you'll ever have: tonno e fagioli, which has tomatoes, okra, and beans in it. It's actually quite tasty!

Da Danilo (Piazza Della Cancelleria 60) is a wonderful spot to grab some of Rome's finest pizza while you're out on the town at night. Go for the pizza Margherita d'oro, which comes decorated with caramelized onions and a bit of fresh mozzarella. The crust here is also quite good. Don't forget to try some of their excellent beer (Birra La Spina).

Locanda delle Coppelle (Via dei Chiavari, 2) has one of the best atmospheres for dinner at night in Rome. This place is small, but it's lively and serves up yummy dishes like risotto al Nero di seppia seafood risotto and sausage agrodolce a few steps from the Trevi Fountain. The red wine is fantastic too — we recommend the Il Sagrantino Sant'Angelo from Abruzzo.

St. Regis Hotel (Via della Croce 12) is a great place to grab a quiet dinner. We recommend the risotto al pomodoro or the spaghetti alla gricia. The portions are large, but you'll still be able to leave satisfied with just a couple of dishes after your meal here.

## Pizza & Pasta

Amaro (Via del Corso, 29) serves up some of the best Italian food in Rome at an affordable price. The pizza al prosciutto and the buffalo mozzarella with mushrooms are our personal favorites. The service is fairly quick, but if you have a large group of people, you might want to call ahead to make sure they can accommodate everyone at once.

You've probably heard of pasta alla carbonara (and maybe even eaten it yourself) before, but do you know what's in it? Basically, the key ingredient here is bacon. It isn't just any bacon—it's the pancetta di San Daniele from Italy. If you want to experience some of the best carbonara in Rome, then we recommend trying this dish at La Carbonara (Via Alessandro Severo, 20). We personally loved the spaghetti alla carbonara here.

Trattoria da Sergio (Via Cecilia Metella, 102) serves up delicious sandwiches, soups, and salads alongside its pasta options. We recommend trying out their spaghetti with meatballs or perhaps a nice little lasagna to fill you up. The service is quick and the portions are large. If you want a meal that's slightly different than the norm, we recommend going here for lunch or dinner.

## Bars & Cafés

Antico Caffè Greco (Piazza di Spagna 26) is one of Rome's oldest cafés and has been open since 1760. It's located right on Piazza di Spagna, and the café is available for diners as well as coffee drinkers. And if you need a quick pick-me-up, this is the place to go for a cappuccino or a pastry.

If you've ever heard of a caffe corretto, then you've probably heard of Antico Caffè Tazza d'Oro (Via degli Orfani 84). This café serves up some of the most famous caffe correttos in Rome. Here's how it works: you order your espresso, but instead of putting sugar in it, you order it with an accompanying liquor like rum or grappa. This way, you get a stronger taste of the liquor in your coffee, and you can even start off with a tiny bit of the drink and slowly build on it. If you want to experience this for yourself, we recommend going to Tazza d'Oro.

Ristorante L'Enoteca (Via dei Coronari, 59) serves up some of the tastiest pastas in Rome. We recommend trying out the gnocchi alla Romana or perhaps their spaghetti carbonara. The portions are large; however, they are not as heavy as some pasta dishes tend to be in Rome. This gives you plenty of room for dessert and perhaps a glass or two of wine to accompany your meal.

## Snacks & Desserts

Rome is home to some of the best gelato that Italy has to offer. For this reason, be sure to grab a cone or two during your stay in the Eternal City. Gelateria Fatamorgana (Via Panisperna, 29) is located right near Rome's Spanish Steps and serves up some of the coolest flavors you'll find anywhere. We recommend picking out a couple of different flavors so you can try them all! These include hazelnut, stracciatella, peanut butter, and chocolate chip cookie dough among others.

This is a perfect spot for snacks and drinks. If you're feeling tired, you can go in here for a quick coffee or some tea. For dessert, you're able to pick out a flavor from the gelato case and have it served on anything from fresh fruit to cookies. It's definitely worth checking this place out!

This gelateria has different flavors of milk, including hazelnut, pistachio, pink fig served with caramel syrup and white chocolate sauce inside. If that's not enough, they also have another flavor available for dessert.

Here you can find the traditional Italian gelato made with quality ingredients. The flavors are very different from what you'll find at the other Italian gelaterias around town, but they still taste fantastic.

This is a great place for rookies in the gelato community. For starters, this shop only takes cash and doesn't take credit cards, which definitely helps cut down on peer-to-peer transactions during dinnertime rushes.

This is one of the few places in town that sells traditional gelato tubs as well as cones.

A real love of gelato has caused Gelatissimo, one of the newer Italian-themed shops to open around town. Their selection of gelato is terrific; however, their choice for cones is rather odd.

They serve only the traditional, tall cone shape that most gelato shops do not carry; rather, they serve short cones that are hardly more than a bite-sized version of the longer ones.

This seems to be an attempt at saving money; however, it means that patrons can scarcely eat half the cone in one sitting.

They also serve tropical fruit and various flavors of ice cream sundaes along with a variety of fruit teas. The prices are decent, but they seem to be a bit high when you consider the size of the servings.

This gelateria has various flavors of milk, including hazelnut, pistachio and pink fig served with caramel syrup and white chocolate sauce. There is also a different flavor available for dessert.

This is one of the few places in town where you can find traditional gelato tubs along with cones. This makes Gelatissimo one of the better places to go where you can eat your gelato on the way home or at work—therefore cutting down on peer-to-peer transactions during dinnertime rushes.

This is one of the few places in Rome where you can find traditional gelato tubs. When you're looking for a treat to eat at home or at work, this makes for an excellent choice. The prices are also quite decent; however, it seems that serving sizes are slightly small when compared to other gelaterias in town.

## Dessert & Treats

Just Gelato (Via dell'Umilta, 6) offers a range of homemade ice creams and sorbets that will make for some excellent treats while you're in the historical center of Rome. The selection of flavors is quite extensive here and you are able to choose your ice cream according to your taste.

Caffè Carlo (Via della Croce, 3) serves up some of the tastiest doughnuts in town. It's located on the Piazza di Spagna, which makes it a pretty convenient spot for a pick-me-up after seeing some of Rome's famous sites in the square. If you're looking for something savory, they also have a few Italian dishes like soup and ravioli.

If you're looking for a quick breakfast while on vacation in Rome, we recommend this place. It's a great little place called Pasticciera la Befana (Via San Teodoro, 21/23). It offers egg breakfasts and meat pizzas. The best part of this experience is that you can eat outside. This is the perfect way to start your day while on vacation or even if it's just one of those days when you need to get out into the fresh air.

This café is famous for its hot chocolate and toast with Nutella. It's located on a quiet street that is 10 minutes from the Pantheon and the Spanish Steps. The atmosphere is very relaxing; however, be aware that there aren't many seats here, so you may have to wait for a table.

Gelateria Castelli (Via dei Colonna, 5) is located right in the center of Rome, at Piazza Navona. This place has traditional Italian gelato flavors as well as some more unusual ones like coffee and chocolate-covered strawberries.

This is a great little place to grab something to eat on the way to or from the Vatican or St. Peter's Basilica in Rome. Though it is not a gelateria, it serves up some of the best pastries and croissants in town. It's located a short walk from either of these famous tourist destinations and only takes cash.

This cafe is located near Piazza di Spagna, so if you're looking for something for lunch or for an afternoon snack on vacation in Rome, this is the place for you. The menu offers combinations of pasta, rice, canapés and salads all served together with their own homemade Italian red vermouth.

This is a perfect spot for snacks and maybe a drink or two. The service is quick and the portion sizes are large. We recommend going here for lunch or dinner if you're looking for something simple and delicious. If you're looking for something savory, check out the salumi plate which offers mini versions of traditional Italian salami like prosciutto, pancetta, coppa to name a few.

# Chapter 6: Rome After Dark

Rome's museums are beautiful, but they're closed after 5 PM. Rome's shops close by 7 PM. And while you might be able to find a few bars and restaurants that are open until midnight, the vast majority of places to have fun in Rome close between 10:30 and 11:00 PM.

You're really not going to find anyplace to have fun at night in Rome after dark.

Besides, the idea of sitting in a restaurant or bar at 10 PM and doing nothing but drinking wine and watching the tourists stagger back to their hotel sounds just awful.

So what's left after dark? There are two areas where Rome's nightlife is still vibrant: clubs and theaters.

But even if you manage to find a club/theater open after dark, they tend to be pretty pricey and do tend towards the "intimate" type of venue. And you can't take your car with you in most cases, so you're stuck with whichever taxi is willing or able to take you home at the end of the evening.

With that in mind, I've come up with a list of five different types of places to have fun after dark in Rome:

## The Roman Pub

This is easily the most popular type of place to hang out after dark in Rome, and one you're almost guaranteed to find. Just walk down any main street on a Friday or Saturday night and you'll see the unmistakable sight of hordes of older tourists walking down the street (usually towards a restaurant or somewhere that serves wine) with locals hanging around outside looking on.

Roman Pubs are like Irish pubs, only they serve beer rather than a stout. And they cater to an older crowd, usually tourists. They are open fairly late and can be a fun place to have some drinks with friends and watch the locals, but you won't "fit in" and you should expect to pay a couple of euros per drink (or more). The two major Roman pubs are:

The Druid's Den, Via di Panico 31 near Piazza Navona (Metro: Flaminio or Piazza del Popolo)

Open from 11:30 AM until 2 or 3 AM on Fridays and Saturdays.

Via della Vite 102, near Termini station but not along any of the main streets.

The Druid's Den is where the "scene" is. You're very likely to run into a high number of tourists mixed in with the locals if you go here, but it's not hard to find an English speaker should you need one. It's also the only Roman pub that I know of that serves alcohol other than beer and wine, including whiskey and other hard liquor.

Via della Vite is a bit more local, but it still attracts quite a few tourists throughout the night.

## Night Clubs

Since the city center is closed to cars, you may have a hard time finding a taxi that's willing/able to take you directly from a nightclub back home. The taxis also tend to be organized into a single line rather than prowling around the streets looking for fares, so if you're going home at 4 AM your only option may be to walk three or four kilometers back home (or pay an extortionate fare).

I would recommend avoiding Rome's nightclubs after 11 PM if you want them to be fun and free of obnoxious foreigners. They also tend to be very expensive, so even if you stay until 4 AM you'll pay a lot for very little.

There's a nightclub called "Kiss" in the Via della Vite area that is quite popular and open until 3 AM or later on Fridays and Saturdays. There are also several nightclubs in the San Lorenzo area (near Stazione di San Lorenzo) that are open until at least 2 AM on weekends.

One tip: nightclubs often don't fill up until around midnight or one a.m., so unless you can get in without paying the cover charge it may be better to wait until later to go.

# The Theater

For culture enthusiasts, there are a number of places to see plays and musicals in Rome. If you've got tickets in hand, then you're all set. If not you can try the Teatro dell'Opera di Roma, which is often open until at least midnight on Fridays and Saturdays. Just be aware that it's usually pretty pricey and gets full quickly, especially if it's a production of an opera or ballet (which are my favorites).

If you want to see a play that's not one of the major ones, there's always the Teatro Massimo in Parioli on Via Appia Antica. It's a bit small and can get quite crowded, but it's one of the few theaters in Rome that serves alcohol. The main drawback is that it isn't open after 11 PM, so you'll have to head back home by 2:30 AM.

# The Dance Hall/Live Music Club/Underground Club/Trance/House/Techno Club

This might just be my favorite type of venue in Rome after dark. The music is different than anything you'll hear at a traditional club. The atmosphere is much more relaxed and friendly. And the cover charge isn't any higher than that at most traditional clubs.

I've had some of the best nights out in my life in Rome at these types of clubs, especially early on a Friday or Saturday night when they're just starting to get going. One warning though: you may not know any of the music here, so if you want to dance with someone (or they want to dance with you) you need to both be on the same page.

Some of my favorite clubs in Rome are:

Alpheus, via dei Serpenti 116 (near Piramide stop on Metro line B). This place has been open since the early 80's and is still going strong. The music is a mix of whatever your DJ or live band feels like playing, from house to reggae to trance, hip hop and everything in between. There's also a sizable sushi buffet in the middle of the dance floor for all you hungry dancers out there.

Anfiteatro delle Milizie, Via Galvani 91 (near San Giovanni stop on Metro line A). This place is housed in an old warehouse that looks like something from the set of an Indiana Jones movie.

In the middle of the dance floor is a giant cage filled with metal bars and giant hoses. It's like being at a rave in an old factory in some post-apocalyptic movie. If you're looking for a place to see some sweaty goths, this is it.

Bio Club, Via Benedetta 21a (just north of Largo di Torre Argentina). A small club located in an old bio-diversity museum (hence the name). Small but full of energy, with some good jazz/funk/soul DJs playing on weekends.

Brancaleone, Via di Monte Testaccio 30 (just south of San Giovanni Metro stop). This place is located on a quiet street in the industrial Testaccio district, which is also home to a collection of funky pubs, great cocktail bars, and lots of restaurants. Brancaleone has two dance floors: the main room is mostly house/trance/techno with a decent-sized crowd; the small back room is usually electro/indie, which I prefer but don't expect to see many others there.

Congress Hall (ex Beehive), Via Ostilia 173 (near San Lorenzo stop on Metro line A). This place looks like it's being used as an anarchist squat. The kind of place that in the past has been targeted by groups of football hooligans.

Eremo, Via di San Pietro 64 (near Lepanto stop on Metro line B). This place is somewhat off the beaten path but worth the extra walk. When you enter, it's a small dark room with a large open dance floor and three bars; one bar is in a corner and one in between the bar and dance floor. The DJ plays mostly house, which is very pleasant to hear in this historic old building.

One of the nice touches is that they have well-placed speakers to provide sound in all parts of the room. The bar and dance floors are on two levels, which is nice to see. Most clubs I've been to either have a bar on the main level or lower level and usually not both.

At this point, you must resist the temptation to get a drink at one of the bars and immediately go out onto one of the balconies with its great view over Rome (on Via di San Pietro). This is my favorite place to be because you really get an idea of Rome's size (which is really big!) and you feel like you're on your own private terrace. It was a beautiful night for it!

# Chapter 7: Drinking and Nightlife

Rome is known for being one of the best places to party, so if you're one for a good time or you're just on vacation, then Rome is your destination. I mean, how could you not be with all of the beautiful art to explore and delicious food that's served everywhere? There are lots of options when it comes to what bars or clubs you want to go to in Rome.

First, there are some of the typical places like "Sputnik" and "B59" that always have pretty crowded nights. These are the places where you can go and be surrounded by other college students who want to just have a good time. However, if you want to get out of the party scene for a little while, then I would definitely recommend checking out some of the nightclubs in Rome.

There is one nightclub, in particular, called "Club Mixx," that has been voted as one of the best places to party in Rome! This club is so famous because it's always full of fun and lively people who love to dance all night long. If you're looking for a place to go and dance, then this is definitely your best bet.

There are also a lot of great restaurants in Rome that cater to tourists so they can have the best food. One restaurant that you might want to check out is called "La Pizzeria." This place is great because it has got a variety of different foods that will definitely fulfill your cravings after all of the walking that you end up doing in Rome. They serve pizzas, salads, pasta, burgers, and even beef ribs! Because where else can you get beef ribs at? They also have some pretty decent appetizers as well like calamari and tapas. So if you're looking for something delicious and a place to go with friends, then this is definitely the place to visit.

Now, you might be wondering what nightclubs or bars there are in Rome that have some live music or other kinds of entertainment. Well, there are a few places where artists come and perform in Rome.

First of all, there's an opera house called "Palazzo Massimo," so if you're into concerts and Italy's culture then this is definitely the place to go to see great Italian singers perform. There are also a couple of theaters where you can see shows and comedians perform. They're called "Teatro Olimpico" and "Teatro Massimo."

When it comes to drinks, few cities can hold a candle to Rome. This is for no other reason than the near-limitless number of bartender talent that exists in the city. The Italian capital may not be a renowned drink-making hub, but every new bar in the Eternal City seems to be making tweaks on old classics as well as inventing new ones.

If you like drinking at night, then Rome is practically heaven on Earth; but how do you know where to start? Don't worry! Here's our guide to drinking and nightlife in Roma with recommendations for great bars and restaurants that'll make your stay one of the most memorable ever.

It's time for a drink in Rome. The Eternal City may not be known for its cocktail scene, but there are quite a few bars and restaurants that offer an excellent selection of drinks, from classic and off-the-beaten-track Italian classics to tried and tested international specialties.

This guide is here to help you navigate these roads less traveled at night.

First thing's first: drink like a Roman in any of the following great spots around the city. But while you're enjoying your drink, make sure to check out some of the best places to take it before or after (or even during) your night out.

Opened in 2014, Da Marra is a hipster-friendly bar/restaurant, offering a selection of craft beers and an international menu. The place is located in the trendy area surrounding Via del Corso (near Piazza Venezia), and it can be a great spot for pre-drinks and dinner or just simply for enjoying some drinks on its nice patio.

We start with the most classic one: Aperol Spritz. It's the most typical drink to have at sunset or early evening and you'll find plenty of bars around Rome doing it right (check out "Santa Monica" near Piazza Venezia).

 What makes a good Spritz? It's the perfect ratio of Aperol, Prosecco and soda, plus the right amount of ice. Enjoy it at Da Marra, one of the best cocktail bars in Rome.

Da Marra is a great place to enjoy your favorite drinks and enjoy some nice music. The bartenders are trained to serve you and they have refined tastes that will make your stay here unforgettable.

If you want to try something experimental, make sure you ask for the Experimental Cocktail List (Liquori e Liquori).

Tips:

- \+ The location is very central but some may not like that it's located in an area full of tourists (near Piazza Venezia).

- \+ In all cases, reserve a table if you want to dine here. They offer more space for your party.

- \+ If you plan on drinking (or eating) just one drink, don't bother ordering a menu at all. Just ask for the Experimental Cocktail List (Liquori e Liquori). You won't regret it! Here are some highlights from the list:

    - Alphaville Martini – A martini with an Aperol twist! Aperol is mixed with dry vermouth and gin in this twist on the classic martini cocktail.

    - Aperol Spritz – A traditional Italian spritzer made with Aperol and Prosecco. The perfect drink for your last night in Rome.

- The Pomegranate Martini – This is a twist on the classics: Granita del Vaticano (made with pomegranate juice) is combined with gin, dry vermouth, and St. Germain elderflower liqueur; served over crushed ice.

- The Bloody Mary – Famous all over the world, this savory drink is a signature item on Da Marra's menu. Made with a blend of spices and tomato juice, it's served over ice with a garnish of fresh herbs and pickled jalapeños.

- The "Morning Glory" Martini – Made with Aperol, house-made vin santo, fresh lemon juice, and soda water. This drink works perfectly at any time of day.

- \+ After a long night out in the center of Rome, nothing beats a good coffee. Da Marra is located in Piazza Venezia, just around the corner from Trastevere (the area to the west of Via del Corso). Walk the seven or eight blocks from Piazza Venezia to Trastevere and you'll find a nice coffee bar, Il Gelato (near the Piazza Santa Maria). You might even want to stop here for the best espresso in Rome (and if you're lucky enough, your barista might even sing for you!).

Well, that was a bit about what to do if you're visiting Rome. I hope that this will help you with your travels.

# Chapter 8: Shopping in Rome

If you're a cultural tourist or just a traveler looking for some great finds, one of the best places for shopping in Rome is on Via dei Condotti. And while every little street in Rome seems to be lined with shops that will tempt you into slowing down to browse their wares, these shops are the cream of the crop.

You'll find everything from high fashion designers such as Valentino and Versace to old-world crafts like handmade paper and hand-painted ceramics.

In other words, you'll never have a better opportunity to spend all your vacation money on beautiful stuff! It's practically impossible not to find something that catches your eye. And while you might not want to drag it all home with you, it's fun just to look.

Keep an eye out for the best deals in designer clothes when Italian fashion houses are having their end-of-season sales. If you've got a taste for the finer things in life, be on the lookout for sale items in stores like Prada and Gucci. You never know what you'll find, but if you're into negotiating for a great deal, you could save a bundle on that designer dress that's just perfect for tonight's big party! These sales usually take place during the summer.

It's possible to find trinkets and souvenirs at almost any time of year. And if you've got an eye for that kind of thing, you'll find that time of the year to be the best time of all.

Shopping in Rome might fall short of Milan's fashion capital, but that doesn't mean there isn't more than enough to see. There are several flagship stores of major retailers such as Zara, Armani, Pinko, and Benetton. You can also find several well-known Italian favorite chains, including La Rinascente, Upim, and Coin. There are many shopping neighborhoods in Rome, and these tend to vary by clientele.

## Piazza di Spagna

While this is an area more known for its iconic Spanish Steps, it is still one of the central shopping districts in Rome. It is where you'll find many flagship stores of luxury brands like Chanel and Louis Vuitton. There's also the famous Sermoneta Gloves where you can find custom-made gloves and a showroom downstairs—very high-end. There are some stores on the side streets as well as galleries and boutiques. Notable stores include The Lion Bookshop with English books and C.U.C.I.N.A specializing in kitchenware and gifts.

## Via Cola di Rienzo

It is a commercial area north of the Vatican and is popular with the locals. It is also a great area to walk and people watch, especially on weekends. It is mostly clothing and fashion stores. The area isn't cheap, but you can find Italian specialties like Castroni, which sells nothing but Italian foods and coffee, making great gifts. There's also a coffee store nearby called Franchi, which has gourmet offerings like real Parmesan cheese, and you can get lunch too. You'll find the Coin department store here, and there's an indoor market here on Sunday mornings as well for fresh foods. It's located across the river from the Piazza del Popolo and can be reached from Metro line A at Lepanto via Marcantonio Colonna.

## Via Del Corso

A family-friendly shopping that also has plenty of small snack bars scattered around, though it's jam-packed with tourists more than locals. It is a slightly cheaper shopping area and great for teenagers. Beware of the "made in Italy" leathers here as many are genuine Italian leather but made in China, which is why the price is so much lower. It is a long shopping road, and you could spend hours here. There's also the Galleria Colonna, a large mall shopping center about halfway up with a cinema.

Nearby both the Cola di Rienzo and del Corso are the Via del Babuino which is high-end jewelry and antique stores. There are also several large boutique stores such as Armani. It's less crowded but pricier. The Via dei Condotti also runs parallel to the del Corso, home to high fashion names like Hermes and Moschino. Other nearby notable streets with shops include the via Frattina, via Della Croce, via Vittoria, Campo de Fiori and the Piazza Navona. The via Nazionale is also a great place to go for budget-friendly shopping.

# Markets

- Mercantino di Villa Glori a Roma – an antique market on the third Sunday of each month is one of the oldest in the city. It is located on the Viale Maresciallo Pilsudski and is only closed in August.

- Mercantino di Ponte Milvio a Roma – probably the most critical flea market in the city. It is held the first and third Sunday of the month except for August and spreads along Capoprati, following the Tiber from the Ponte Milvio. The bridge is beautiful in itself, and there's also a lovely green park as a setting. There are over 150 stalls, and it's always busy.

- Campo dei Fiori – every morning except Sundays, this is a local food market that is very colorful and is also the most well-known in the city since it has been running since 1869.

- Campagna Amica – near the circus Maximus the market has a strict kilometer rating, so all goods are made locally. It is the perfect place to get oils, olives, cheeses, and other "Italian" only gifts.

# What to Buy

## Clothes

Italy is known for its fashion, and the Via Condotti is the place to go to Rome for clothes shopping. Think of Italian silk scarves, brightly patterned and delicate. These are a popular choice as they can also be found cheap by street vendors and make ideal gifts.

## Leather Goods

Italian leather is also a good choice as you can find bags and shoes made there. These are of outstanding value, and you'll also find large replica pieces that are higher quality genuine leather than those from China. These goods are usually fun to haggle over, especially with street vendors.

## Jewelry

Ancient Romans priced jeweled items, and the tradition has persisted today, and the gold jewelry you can find now is usually unique and elegant. Alternatively, there is also plenty of exciting galleries selling unique designs and costume jewelry instead.

## Glass

Murano Glass is technically not from the area (it's made in Venice), but it's still easy to find. Make sure it's accurate as not all glass is authentic Murano, and there are plenty of imitations—always ask for the certificate since there will always be one for actual items. Murano glass comes in a massive selection of colors and designs and is very high quality.

## Food

Depending on where you're traveling from, you can bring food home with you. Dairy tends to be an issue in and out of the E.U., so be careful if you're buying Parmesan. Parma ham (while technically from Parma) and Genoa Salami are also popular choices within the E.U. and fall under the "meat and dairy" import rules. Other choices that are safer include olive oil, balsamic vinegar, and chocolate. You'll find many boutique-side stores selling things like this all over the city.

# Chapter 9: Rome with Kids

If you're going to Rome with kids, there are a couple of things you must know.

First and foremost, the city has so much for kids to see and do! So ensure that they have a good itinerary planned out ahead of time.

And don't be surprised if your children turn down visiting major historical sites—kids aren't born with the knowledge that the Colosseum is a symbol of Roman power or that Vatican City housed the Pope until relatively recently, so they may not be interested in these sites.

## Best Museums & Sites for Kids

Explora: Museo dei Bambini di Roma (%06 361 37 76; Via Flaminia 80-86; €8, children 1-3yr €5, under 1yr free; entrance 10 am, noon, 3 pm & 5 pm Tue-Sun, no 10 am entrance in Aug; Flaminio).

Rome's only dedicated kids' museum, Explora is aimed at the under-12s.

It's divided into thematic sections, and with everything from a play pool and fire engine to a train driver's cabin, it's a hands-on, feet-on, full-on experience that your nippers will love.

Outside there's also a free play park open to all. Booking is recommended for the timed entrance and is required on weekends.

Bioparco (%06 360 82 11; Viale del Giardino Zoologico 1; adult/reduced €16/13; h9.30am-6 pm summer, to 5 pm winter; Bioparco) Rome's zoo hosts a predictable collection of animals, with 200 species from five continents housed on its 18-hectare site in Villa Borghese.

Museo Delle Cere (Wax Museum; %06 679 64 82; www.museodellecereroma.com; Piazza Dei Santissimi Apostoli 68a; adult/reduced €10/8; h 9 am – 9 pm summer, to 8 pm winter; c) Rome's waxwork museum is said to have the world's third-largest collection, which comprises more than 250 figures, ranging from Dante to Snow White, plus plentiful popes, poets, politicians, musicians, and murderers. Don't miss the laboratory where the waxworks are created.

## Top Tips

- Under-18s get in free at state-run museums.

- City-run museums are free for under-sixes and discounted for six to 25-year-olds.

- Under-10s travel free on public transport.

# Chapter 10: Travel Tips

## Arriving in Rome

### Leonardo da Vinci – Fiumicino Airport

You'll arrive about 18 miles from the city center; it's one of the busiest in Europe and was opened in 1961. There are three passenger terminals divided into regional airlines, budget airlines, and long haul.

An express train takes 30 minutes to Termini station, non-stop, twice an hour, and the local trains head to Trasvestere, Ostiense, or Tuscolana. There are also several buses from the city to the airport.

## Civitavecchia

Cruise ships that stop in "Rome" will dock here outside the city itself. You can only reach Rome from the town by train or by hiring a car. Occasionally cruise lines will charter a dedicated bus, but it's not common. From the train, you'll arrive at the central Termini station in an hour on the regional train or the fast interCity train, which takes 45 minutes.

## Ciampino Airport

There are several shuttle connections between the Termini station and this smaller airport, though the routes are crowded, and it can be up to two hours since the buses are not regular. Casabianca station is a little walk from the airport and is often a better choice though it's not ideal for pedestrians, so a taxi is advised. The station has a direct train into Rome Termini.

# Getting Around

Public transport in Rome costs €1.50 per single ticket and must be used within 100 minutes of purchase. There are also seven-day passes valid for the metro, buses, trams, and trains inside municipal Rome for €24, including unlimited trips, a 24-hour pass for €7 and a three-day pass for €12.50. If you're staying for an extended time, consider a monthly pass that can be renewed using a €10 renewable card, the month pass itself is €35 and can be bought at any metro station. Children under ten travel free on public transport, and routes do change for nights and weekends, so check before traveling at these times.

A good option for visitors is the three-day Roma Pass (€35) which offers unlimited travel and includes discounted entry for a wide variety of museums and monuments and another for €28 which lasts for two days.

The pass also allows for one museum free in 24 hours or 2 in 3 days in addition to these.

## Metro

While most of Rome is foot accessible, it also has an extensive underground railway system to get across town quickly. The metro has three lines, though the B line splits from Bologna to Jonio.

A and B lines run in an X formation across the city, intersecting at the main Termini Station. Line C is primarily a suburban line that doesn't intersect with most sightseeing routes or connect with any other lines.

As with most urban underground systems, it can be extremely crowded during rush hour, and you should always be aware of pickpockets. The original network only dates back to 1955, and there are plans for a fourth-line eventually. It's also called the ATAC after the operating company.

## Tram & Buses

Rome has an extensive network of trams and buses, which can be helpful when getting between two sights as it can reach most within a stop or two on overground transport. There are mini electric-bus routes that specifically go to the tourist sites only as well. The central bus station is in front of Termini station.

As the buses aren't always prompt, thanks to traffic, you may want to check the route and see if whatever arrives is going in that direction and arriving close instead of waiting. Buses run between 5.30 am and midnight, as well as several night services on main routes.

In central Rome, where many ancient ruins are, there are no metro or train lines, and the bus will be your only option unless you want to walk. These are always crowded, and people are known to be pushy and rude when getting on.

These are the most common tourist routes:

40 (Limited stop express) - Termini - Piazza Venezia - Argentina - Piazza Pia (for St Peter's/Vatican)

64 - Termini - Piazza Venezia - Argentina - Vatican

62 - Repubblica - Spanish Steps - Piazza Venezia - Argentina - Vatican

81 - Vatican Museums - Piazza Imperatore (Spanish Steps) - Piazza Colonna (Trevi Fountain) - Piazza Venezia - Circo Massimo - Colosseum

60 - Termini - Piazza Venezia - Colosseum - Circo Massimo

H - Termini - Piazza Venezia - Argentina - Trastevere

8 (Tram) - Piazza Venezia - Argentina - Trastevere

Rome also has a network of Hop-on Hop-off buses that offer multiple different tours. These are good for families who may have children who like to ride on the open-top and see the sights rather than going in. There are several companies, and some also have circuit routes that do not stop.

- Big Bus Rome

    Cheapest ticket: 24 hours, €25.50/adult

    Websites state free for children age four and under

- I Love Rome Hop on Hop off Panoramic Tour (run by Gray Line)

    Cheapest ticket: 24 hours, €25.73/adult

    "Single ride" ticket (no hop on, hop off) €16.37/adult

    The website indicates free for children age five and under

- Open Tour Bus

    Cheapest ticket: 24 hours "online special" €17.99/adult

    The website states free for children age five and under "if they do not occupy a seat."

- GreenLine Panoramic Open Tour

    One Day (online web special, not 24 hours) €15/adult

    "One runs no stop" ticket (no hop on, hop off) €12/adult

The website states free for children age five and under

- Roma Christiana Bus (note, this bus route includes some additional stops)

    One Day (not 24 hours) €20/adult

    "One full circuit" ticket (no hop on, hop off) €12/adult

    Note: website states free for children age nine and under and for individuals with disabilities, recommend a contact in advance as to what documentation may be required for a free ticket

Terravision also operates a regular bus service to the airports from the Termini station.

## Taxis

These are not recommended as most of Rome suffers from terrible traffic congestion, and you'll spend most of your time stuck. It makes this the most expensive travel option and should only be used for longer journeys where no other transit is available or to the airports.

There is a fixed rate for up to 4 people that most companies offer to and from the airport to hotels within the city walls of about €30.

Some may charge for bags but do not pay more than €1 per bag. Do not accept rides from taxis that are not on an official taxi rank, as many unlicensed private vehicles are sketchy.

There have also been reports of drivers swapping €50 for €10 notes which look similar, arguing that that is what you gave them. Official taxis are white with a taxi sign on the roof and the Rome crest on the doors fitted with a meter. Please make sure they use the meter too, or you may end up overpaying. It is not necessary to tip, but it is common practice to round up the change.

## Walking

In the central area of Rome, this is often the only choice as buses are not always fast and many attractions are close together. There are many walking tours of the city available if you don't want to make your own.

GPS offers 39 different free walking tours you can follow to see everything in Rome.

## Bike Share

Rome has a bike-share program, but considering how difficult the roads are to navigate and how crowded, this isn't necessarily a good choice. You can get registered for the bikes at any ATAC center where you'll get a smartcard. It can then be topped up and costs you €5. Every 30 minutes you have the bike, your card will be charged €1, and return the bike to any station within 4 hours. There are share points across the city, including at several prominent attractions like the Pantheon.

Rome can certainly be done in 5-7 days if you plan on seeing the main attractions only. A couple of days more is suggested for those who want to add more religious choices or who have a desire to see the more out-of-the-way sights. You can also make a day trip to Pompeii from Rome quite easily.

# Shopping and Sights. 7 days

Day 1: Vatican and Borgo

Start your day with an early stroll through the Vatican gardens, and then walk your way to the Vatican Museums. You'll spend around 3 hours touring the museums before walking back across the gardens to the Sistine Chapel. It's a good idea to grab a packed lunch for today since there isn't anywhere to eat here, and the gardens are lovely to relax in while you eat. Then head out to dinner and an early night.

Day 2: Roman Rome

Get up early and head straight to the Colosseum to avoid the queues. Take one of the walking tours. From here, walk the 1/5km to the Roman Forum. After visiting the Forum, head to the Piazza Venezia to see the architecture and enjoy lunch at one cafe.

Day 3: Parks and Piazzas

Start your day at the Galleria Borghese set in the Villa Borghese grounds (don't forget to get tickets in advance). After you're done with the museum, tour the villa and park. From here, walk to the National Gallery of Ancient Art and see the massive selection of artifacts.

Day 4: Shopping and Baroque Sightseeing

Start the day at the Via Cola di Rienzo to visit the high-end fashion district and boutique stores. Grab lunch here as well. After lunch, head over to the Altar of peace across the river and see an ancient Roman sculpture from the first-century ad.

Day 5: Roman Baths and Trasvestere

Start your day at the beautiful church of Santa Maria in Trasvestere. Enjoy the beautiful interior in peace before heading to Santa Cecilia for similar Baroque architecture but a very different interior. After you're done, quickly get to the Porta Portese. You'll see a city gate from the 17th century, which is often called the 8th hill of Rome.

Day 6: The Appian Way and Rome's Catacombs

You'll be walking along part of the Appian Way today, and if you'd rather avoid the gruesome catacombs, you can swap to walking the entire route instead. Start your Day at the Catacombs of St Domitilla and enjoy contrasting with how white and pristine these are compared to the others you will see.

Day 7: Galleries and Museums

Start the Day at the National Etruscan Museum located in a stately Renaissance villa. Walk to the National Gallery of Modern Art and enjoy lunch at the park nearby afterward. Enjoy the park scenery as you walk to the Museo Carlo Bilotti.

Currency: euro (€)

Language: Italian

Visas: Generally not required to stay of up to 90 days.

Money: ATMs are widespread. Major credit cards are widely accepted, but smaller businesses might not take them.

Mobile Phones: Can use local SIM cards in European, Australian, and unlocked US phones. Must set other phones to roaming.

Time: Western European Time (GMT/UTC plus one hour)

Not necessary, but round the bill up in pizzerias/trattorias or leave a euro or two; five to 10% is acceptable in more innovative restaurants.

## Book Your Stay

Rome is expensive and busy; book your accommodation ahead to secure the best deal.

Accommodation options range from palatial five-star hotels to hostels, B&Bs, pensioni, and private rooms; there's also a growing number of boutique suites and apartment hotels.

Everyone overnight in Rome pays the Tassa di soggiorno, a room-occupancy tax on top of their bill: €3 per person per night in one- and two-star hotels; €3.50 in B&Bs and room rentals; €4/6/7 in three-/four-/five-star hotels.

When you check into your accommodation, you'll need to present your passport or identification card.

# Conclusion

Rome, Italy is one of the most visited cities in the world, but its history extends back to almost 2,000 BC. The city has captivated and fascinated visitors for decades and continues to be a wealth of culture, art, and architecture.

Yes, it can be difficult to get around Rome if you don't have an Italian guide or are struggling to understand the language; but with this list of places to visit while in Rome there's no excuse not to prolong your vacation by taking time off for yourself.

If you're dreaming of exploring Rome, then get ready to do just that and more in this! It's all here in one place; so read on if you want to know everything!

1) Choose Your Travel Dates Wisely: There are many reasons why people visit Rome throughout the year, so it's important that you pick a good date before booking

your flight. If you are planning to visit in the summer, for example, it's not a good idea to visit in the middle of winter. The city is much warmer during this time so let the hotels know before booking your place there.

2) Book Your Flight: Most of us prefer to plan our vacations beforehand and have everything all worked out ahead of time, but keep in mind that Rome isn't exactly like other destinations around the world. For instance, if you want a stopover in Rome on your way back home, you cannot do that with your flight. You have to book everything prior to purchase. So, keep that in mind if you would like a stopover when booking for Rome travel.

3) Rent Your Car: If you're planning on driving yourself around Rome, then you can look into renting a car instead of using public transportation. You'll be saving some money and making your trip much more enjoyable by doing this. The train and subway are terrible during peak hours and taxis are quite expensive as well; so it's best to rent a car if you can afford it.

4) Check the Weather: Traveling in Italy during the summer season can be quite a challenge. The country is much hotter and this puts some strain on the outdoor infrastructure; so be sure to check out the weather before you go! It's best to visit in May or September if you can.

5) Visit Nearby Attractions: Rome has a lot of amazing attractions that are not really within walking distance from each other. So, if you've got limited time, then splurge and save your money by renting a car or taxi and driving yourself around! This will get you to one place from another in no time at all. You may have to do this for a few days, so be sure to budget for it!

6) If You'd Like to See the Colosseum: You can't miss it while in Rome! Just make sure you keep an eye out for the signs and make your way there. The Roman Colosseum is not very far away from Via Cavour, which will be on your left as you head towards the Terme di Caracalla.

7) Walk Through Trastevere: There are many great places around this neighborhood worth seeing. One such place is the Basilica of Sant'Eusebio; which is just a short walk from Piazza di Campitelli. There's also a very interesting church nearby called Santa Prisca. Both of these places are great for exploring.

8) Visit the Spanish Steps: The Spanish steps will not be far away from your hotel once you arrive in Rome. This is a great way to see some culture while in Rome and you can't miss it while there!

9) Take Advantage of the Free Museums: In Rome, there are tons of museums that are free to visit throughout

the year. There are so many museums in this city that offer free admission that just walking through the Roman Forum would take you forever! Rome has some of the coolest museums in the world, so be sure to check them out!

10) Eat at a Trattoria: You must eat at a trattoria while you're in Rome; if you don't, you're missing something great! They are usually located close together; so it's easy to get around. There's one in Piazza Navona and one on Via dei Condotti. The only thing is that it's hard to find a nice trattoria in the touristy areas of Rome.

11) Don't Forget to Visit the Colosseum: If you're in Rome, you've got to see the ancient ruins of the Roman Colosseum. It's one of the Seven Wonders of the World; so how could you resist?

12) Get Your Hands on Some Gelato: Gelato is not always easy to find around here, but there are plenty of vendors who sell it very close to sites like Trevi Fountain or near Piazza Navona while others will try to sell this treat at street level by various attractions around town. There are many gelato stand vendors that you'll be able to find.

13) Eat at a Pizza Restaurant: Rome is known for its pizzas and has some of the best pizzas in the whole world!

There are tons of amazing pizza shops all around Rome, so enjoy the Italian treat while there.

14) Purchase a Roman Photo Pass: You can purchase a discounted photo pass in Rome that includes more than 100 pictures taken by local photographers and those that include great angles and great backgrounds. This is perfect if you're looking for something unique to take pictures of while in Rome and this way you don't have to hire an official photographer.

15) Explore the Natural Parks: There are some beautiful parks throughout Rome. Plus, these parks will provide you with a beautiful view to take pictures of.

16) Take a Bus Tour: You can easily take a bus tour in the main tourist areas of Rome. There are many tours to choose from and they all offer you a good time while visiting the city. So, grab one while you're there and get around!

17) Visit the Pantheon: This temple is one of the most famous churches in Rome, so it's well worth trying to visit it at least once while you're there. It's located close by to Piazza di Spagna; so be sure to stop by if you want to see the outside of this place. It's a beautiful structure that is not too far from your hotel.

18) Take a Selfie with the Colosseum: This is a must-do thing while in Rome; you've got to take a picture with the iconic Colosseum! There are tons of photo opportunities that you can take while at this place; so don't forget to take pictures of it while there.

19) Walk Around the Spanish Steps: The Piazza di Spagna is one of the most popular spots in all of Rome. It is filled with shops, restaurants, and hotels as well as tourists. Just be sure to walk around and check out this area because it's worth taking the time to do so.

20) Visit the Roman Forum: This is the famous marketplace in Rome where all the senators would meet and transact business. The building is impressive and so is walking around it! It's located a few miles from Vatican City; so be sure to stop by if you want to check it out while you're in Rome.

21) Buy Souvenirs at Bourbon Street: There are tons of souvenir shops that sell anything from jewelry to shirts, so if you're looking for some unique souvenir while in Rome, check out some of these places. They are a few miles from your church; so stop by if you want to see the shops and sites while in Rome.

22) Visit the Trevi Fountain: This is one of the most famous fountains in Rome, so be sure to take some pictures with it while there.

23) Visit the Coliseum as Well as Palatino Hill: The Colosseum is stunning; but for those who want more history, this might be something you want to see too.

24) Visit the Pantheon: This is another of the most famous temples in Rome.

25) Visit The Spanish Steps: This is a famous hill located off the Piazza di Spagna.

26) Visit the Vatican Museums: You can make this a full day, but I'd suggest getting there before 9 am to avoid crowds. You will be able to see and visit all of these museums in one day if you want; here's how I recommend you spend your time there: Piazza Navona - Vittoriano - Barcaccia Museum - Roman Forum - Galleria Borghese - Palatino Hill - Pantheon - Capitoline Museum. Includes admission to the Vatican Museums. Tour must be taken in one day and is only available on Tuesdays.

The best way to see Rome, which includes a guided tour of one main area of the city, plus an extended guided tour of two other areas of the city.

This tour offers guests a private guide and an air-conditioned vehicle for 4 hours. Pick-ups can be arranged at any hotel or address in Rome booked by Iberiabroad.com, and tours in other languages are available upon request (extra charge may apply).

A map and information about public transportation will be provided during your trip to allow you to explore on your own afterward if you wish.

This is a good tour if you want to see some of the main attractions in Rome. It includes both the historical and the modern areas of the city, so you are allowed to get a taste of both during your trip.

This tour is perfect for first-time visitors who would like a more comprehensive overview of Rome, or for those who want to revisit this amazing city as well.

What are you waiting for? The best time is now!

# Appendix: Rome Metro (Subway) Map

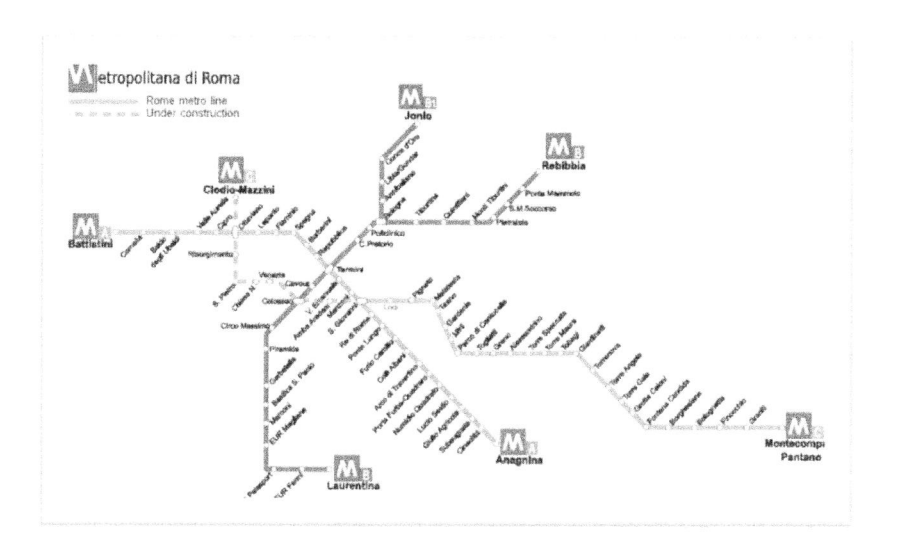

Printed in Great Britain
by Amazon